D0432075

# Amazing Animal Defenses

## Animals with
# Crafty Camouflage
### Hiding in Plain Sight

Susan K. Mitchell

**Enslow Publishers, Inc.**
40 Industrial Road
Box 398
Berkeley Heights, NJ 07922
USA

http://www.enslow.com

*These books are dedicated to Emily, who inspired the author.*

**Library of Congress Cataloging-in-Publication Data**
Mitchell, Susan K.
 Animals with crafty camouflage : hiding in plain sight / by Susan K. Mitchell.
     p. cm. — (Amazing animal defenses)
 Includes bibliographical references and index.
 Summary: "Readers will find out about animals who blend in with their surroundings to avoid predators"—Provided by publisher.
 ISBN 978-0-7660-3291-0
 1. Camouflage (Biology)—Juvenile literature. I. Title.
 QL759.M58 2009
 591.47'2—dc22

                    2008011073

ISBN-10: 0-7660-3291-4

Printed in the United States of America

10 9 8 7 6 5 4 3 2 1

**To Our Readers:**
We have done our best to make sure all Internet Addresses in this book were active and appropriate when we went to press. However, the author and the publisher have no control over and assume no liability for the material available on those Internet sites or on other Web sites they may link to. Any comments or suggestions can be sent by e-mail to comments@enslow.com or to the address on the back cover.

♻ Enslow Publishers, Inc., is committed to printing our books on recycled paper. The paper in every book contains 10% to 30% post-consumer waste (PCW). The cover board on the outside of each book contains 100% PCW. Our goal is to do our part to help young people and the environment too!

**Cover photo:** iStockphoto/Auke Holwerda
**Interior photos:** Alamy/Andre Seale, p. 16; Alamy/B. Mete Uz, p. 18; Alamy/Organica, p. 19; Alamy/Wolfgang Kaehler, p. 20 (right); Alamy/Rolf Nussbaumer, p. 26; Alamy/Bryan & Cherry Alexander Photography, p. 27; Alamy/Kevin Schafer, p. 37 (top and bottom); Alamy/Richard Cooke, p. 43 (bottom); Animals Animals–Earth Scenes/Breck P. Kent, p. 9; Animals Animals–Earth Scenes/Anthony Bannister, p. 20 (left); Animals Animals–Earth Scenes/Mark Chappell, p. 25; Arctic Photo/Frank Todd, p. 23; Fotolia/Rico Leffanta, p. 12; Fotolia/Ozgur, p. 15; The Image Works/Michael J. Doolittle, pp. 28, 33; The Image Works/Topham, p. 42; iStockphoto/Auke Holwerda, p.1; iStockphoto/Kenneth O'Quinn, p. 8; iStockphoto/Yang Lee, p. 10; iStockphoto/Yurii Gorulko, p. 11; iStockphoto/Stephan Hoerold, p. 36; iStockphoto/Nico Smit, p. 38; Minden Pictures/Mitsuhiko Imamori, p. 7; Minden Pictures/Piotr Naskrecki, p. 31; Minden Pictures/Stephen Dalton, p. 40; Shutterpoint Photography/William O'Hara, p. 4; Shutterpoint Photography/Espen M. Knutsen, p. 34; U.S. Department of Defense/Robbin Cresswell, U.S. Air Force, p. 43 (top); U.S. Marine Corps/Cpl. R. Drew Hendricks, p. 44; Visuals Unlimited/Theo Allofs, p. 24; Visuals Unlimited/Joe McDonald, p. 32.

# Contents

# Chapter 1 Hide and Seek

In the animal world, standing out in a crowd can be a bad thing. If an animal is noticed, it might become lunch! To keep from becoming a meal, many animals hide in plain sight. This is called camouflage.

Having good camouflage means that an animal can blend in with the world around it.

**This owl's feathers help it to blend in with the trees where it spends most of its time.**

Some animals use their color to hide. Other animals can use both their color and the bumpy, scaly, rough, or smooth texture of their skin, feathers, or fur. There are many ways an animal can use camouflage. Some animals are born with camouflage. Their coloring naturally blends in with their environment. Other actually change color to match their surroundings.

Some animals have stripes or spots to blend in with the shadows. Others have bodies that look like the plants around them. Still others can change their shape. All of these animals have one thing in common. Their camouflage has changed to become better and better over a very long period of time.

## It's Only Natural

Good camouflage can take many, many years to develop. This means that over time, the

5

animals with the best disguises win! The better an animal blends in with its world, the less likely it is to be eaten. The animal may even live long enough to have babies. Then, it will pass its successful camouflage on to its young. In contrast, an animal with not-so-good camouflage is more likely to die before it can have babies. Scientists call this natural selection.

Camouflage is always changing. As the world around an animal changes, so does the way it hides itself. What helped an animal

**Wild FACT** **Some predators also use camouflage! This allows them to sneak up on their prey without being seen.**

hide at one time might not work anymore if its surroundings change. One good example of this change is the peppered moth.

Before the nineteenth century, almost all of the peppered moths in England were pale

**Looking like leaves is a great disguise for this rain forest moth.**

with dark specks. This helped them hide on trees covered in lichens. Lichens are light-colored organisms that grow on the trunks of some trees. Very few peppered moths had dark wings.

The Industrial Revolution changed this. Many factories were built in England's cities. They used coal to power their machines. The coal made the air become dirty. This resulted in fewer lichens growing on trees in the cities, so the trees looked darker.

# A Colorful Mood

**The chameleon** is a lizard that is known for its cool camouflage. It can change its skin to almost any color. This helps it blend in to match its surroundings. If it is among the leaves of a tree, it can be bright green. When it moves to darker areas, it can become brownish or even black. Special cells in the chameleon's skin help it to change color.

The chameleon's color changes are not only for hiding. For example, an angry chameleon has bright red or orange skin. A chameleon can even turn cool blues or yellows when it is content. Its skin can also turn different colors, which sometimes form a pattern.

The light-colored peppered moth is better camouflaged than the dark one on this light-colored tree.

Scientists noticed that the number of dark-winged peppered moths started growing. However, the dark moths were only found near the cities. Out in the country, where the air was cleaner, lichens still grew. In this area, there were still more light-colored moths. The more a peppered moth matched its environment, the more likely it was to survive.

## Dyeing to Fit In

No matter what color animals are, they have one thing in common—pigment cells. These special cells control the color of skin. In people, these cells make a chemical called melanin. The color of a person's skin depends on the amount of melanin he or she has. More melanin means darker skin, while less melanin means lighter skin.

Many animals have skin that is covered in fur or feathers. Fur and feathers also have pigment cells. The pigment cells in an animal's skin, along with those in its fur or feathers, help determine what color the animal is.

**Wild FACT** There are some animals that are born with no pigment. This is called albinism. Albinism can happen in many different types of animals. Albino animals are white with pink eyes. Because they do not have the camouflage of other members of their species, they usually do not survive in the wild.

**Fur and skin work together to make an animal a certain color and pattern.**

For many animals, their color makes the perfect disguise. For example, if an animal lives among leaves, being green is very helpful. Brown animals that live around dirt or tree bark can also easily hide. These animals blend into the world around them thanks to their crafty camouflage!

11

## Chapter 2

## Underwater Illusionist

The octopus can teach us a thing or two about camouflage. Few animals can disguise themselves like an octopus can. Its skin can change color to match almost anything. It can even change from smooth to rough and bumpy. The octopus has some of the most amazing camouflage of any animal.

Octopuses are found all over the world. They can live in warm waters, icy seas, and everywhere in between. Most octopuses live in

**To blend in with its surroundings, an octopus's skin can turn splotchy and bumpy.**

shallow water along the shore. A few of them can live in deeper water.

There are more than one hundred different types of octopus. Some are very tiny. The pygmy octopus is not much more than an inch long. Others are gigantic. The giant Pacific octopus can grow to be more than 15 feet long. That is half as long as a school bus! Big or small, all octopuses have the ability to change color and hide.

## Who Are You Calling Spineless?

Octopuses are very shy creatures. An octopus is more likely to swim away than fight. All octopuses are in the same animal group as squid. They are called cephalopods (SEF-a-low-pods). "Cephalopod" is a Greek word. Cephalo- means "head" and -pod means "foot." That is pretty much what an octopus looks like—eight long "feet" attached to a head. (The "feet" are actually called arms, however.)

Inside an octopus's head is a very smart brain. Octopuses are thought to be the smartest of all invertebrates, which are animals that have no backbone. Octopuses in science labs have been trained to do many things. Some have learned to swim through mazes. Others have learned how to use their arms to open jars of shrimp.

Wriggling under the head are eight long arms. Each of an octopus's arms is lined with two rows of suction cups. These are used to

**Wild FACT** **Octopuses are super messy! They often leave piles of shells and other leftovers from their meals outside the door of their den.**

catch food and for movement. An octopus uses its arms and suction cups to help it crawl along the ocean floor. The arms can zap out and grab prey as it passes by the octopus's den. They can also feel along the ocean floor for food.

14

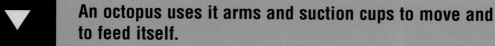

An octopus uses it arms and suction cups to move and to feed itself.

## Disappearing Act

An octopus looks like lunch to many ocean animals. For example, octopuses are a favorite food of some large eels. Dolphins and sharks like to eat octopuses also.

An octopus does not always have time to get away from a predator. Sometimes there are no nearby places for the octopus to hide. The only thing it can do is try to disappear.

15

# Extreme Underwater Makeover

Not all animals are lucky enough to have natural camouflage. That does not stop the decorator crab. It takes things from its surroundings and makes its own camouflage.

These crafty crabs will use just about anything they can get their claws on for camouflage. They take bits of seaweed or coral and hook them on their legs and shells. They even use bits of sponge and small sea creatures called anemones (a-NEM-o-nees). Decorator crabs sometimes pile on so much that they can barely be seen under their decorations. This helps them look more like a moving rock than food!

The octopus can blend in with almost any background. Millions of special skin cells help the octopus change colors. Each of these cells can change color independently of the others.

The amount and type of color released determines what color the octopus will turn. How the octopus does this is a bit of a mystery. Do octopuses see their surroundings and change colors to fit in? Not necessarily. Scientists have studied blind octopuses that are still able to perfectly blend in with their surroundings.

The color changes can happen very fast. An octopus can change colors in less than a second. Patterns of color can also form on its skin. This comes in handy since most surfaces are not one solid color.

Camouflage is not the only reason that an octopus turns colors. Like a chameleon, an octopus's color can show its mood. It is possible to tell by their skin color whether some kinds of octopuses are afraid, angry, or relaxed.

Researchers have seen octopuses turning red when bothered. Others have been seen turning white when frightened.

Octopuses do not just change colors. Even the texture of their skin can change. An octopus's skin is normally smooth. But special muscles in the skin can make the octopus look bumpy like a rock, or grainy like sand. This helps it blend in even better with its surroundings. It also helps make the octopus the true underwater camouflage champion.

Super-bumpy skin helps hide an octopus against the rough ocean floor.

# The Invisible Fish

There are a few animals in the ocean who have some very strange camouflage. They do not change color like an octopus. They do not have skin that looks like rocks or sand. Instead, they are practically invisible.

Certain types of shrimp, as well as the glass catfish (above), are examples of animals with clear, see-through bodies. This is a wonderful disguise. To other animals, they look like reflected light in the water. Whatever surface the animal lands on shows right through it. It can look like the sand, rocks, or plants around it just by staying still.

## Chapter 3

## Seasons of Change

Many animals live in habitats that change regularly. Because of this, there are times when their camouflage no longer works. That is especially true in the snowy Arctic. During much of the year, the Arctic is covered in white. There are months, however, when the snow melts away. During that time, the land turns shades of brown and green. The mammals and birds that live in the Arctic

**The camouflage of arctic hares and other arctic animals helps them stay hidden, no matter the season.**

have developed a special type of camouflage. They can change from brown to white and back again with the changing seasons.

The Arctic is the name for the far northern areas of the earth. Places such as Greenland, Alaska, and parts of Russia and Canada are considered arctic regions.

Life in the Arctic is extremely tough. The temperatures there stay near or below freezing most of the year. The yearly average temperature in many arctic areas is just 7 degrees Fahrenheit. Even the summers are quite cold. The temperature barely gets above freezing (32 degrees Fahrenheit). Often the temperature is only just high enough to melt some of the snow.

There are many different kinds of animals living in these icy places. Some are hunters. Some are hunted. They have all learned, however, to survive in the Arctic.

21

One animal that definitely needs to rely on camouflage to survive is the collared lemming.

## Surviving in the Snow

Lemmings are tiny mammals called rodents. This group also includes hamsters, beavers, and mice. There are many different types of lemmings. The collared lemming, however, is the only one who can grow a coat of white fur.

The collared lemming's small size makes it the perfect meal for many arctic predators. If spotted by a predator, the collard lemming will often seek safety under the snow in a burrow.

A hiding place under the snow does not sound very warm, but a lemming's snowy burrow is actually quite comfortable! The collard lemming lines its burrow with grasses

**Wild FACT** Collard lemmings are not the only arctic animals that grow winter white coats. The arctic hare and a type of weasel called a stoat also turn snowy white in winter.

A collared lemming in its brown summer coat peeks out of a burrow.

and bits of fur. This makes a cozy nest for the lemming. It also provides a safe place to hide.

When they are not resting in their burrows, collard lemmings search in the snow for food. Coming out into the open is dangerous. Unlike some animals, lemmings do not hibernate during the winter. They are active all year long. This means they are in danger of being eaten all year long as well. They rely on their coat of fur for camouflage.

23

# After You, My Dear!

Fur is not the only thing turning white in the Arctic. Arctic birds sprout white feathers each winter. The ptarmigan (TAR-mi-gan) is one of the few birds who can live in the cold Arctic.

Most arctic animals change their fur or feathers at the same time as others of the same species. The rock ptarmigan does things a little differently. It has a "ladies first" rule. Both the males and females grow their winter white feathers at the same time. When spring comes, the male stays white, while the female begins to grow out her brownish feathers. They are the perfect camouflage in the brown arctic grass.

Scientists think the male does this in order to keep other animals away from the female. Since the male is now very visible with his white feathers against the brown grass, predators are more likely to see and go after him. Meanwhile, the female stays hidden as she takes care of her eggs. After a while, the male finally grows his brown summer feathers, too (right).

**Being white in the winter makes hunting for food a little safer for the collared lemming.**

## Winter Whites

In the summer months, the collared lemming grows grayish-brown fur. It has a lighter stripe of fur around its neck that looks like a collar. This is where the collared lemming gets its name. In the winter, the collared lemming grows new, white fur. It is the perfect camouflage for living in the snow.

Fur, hair, and feathers are not made up of living cells. They cannot change from one color to another like skin can. So, the collared lemming has to grow completely new fur.

25

# Going Green in the Rain Forest

The Amazon rain forest in South America is the exact opposite of the Arctic. It is extremely wet and hot. Animals in the rain forest, however, face just as much danger as arctic animals. Things can be especially dangerous for an animal that moves as slowly as the sloth!

The sloth spends most of its life hanging upside down in trees. It has few defenses against predators. A speedy getaway is definitely not possible. So, the sloth depends on camouflage to blend in with the trees.

The sloth has a naturally brownish-gray coat. In the rainy season, however, a thick green coating of tiny plants called algae grows on the sloth's fur. It actually makes the sloth look green. Since a sloth moves so slowly, the algae is able to easily grow and thrive. This greenish-colored fur helps the sloth hide in the rain forest trees.

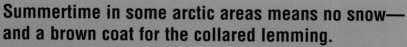

**Summertime in some arctic areas means no snow— and a brown coat for the collared lemming.**

As winter gets closer, the days get shorter and colder. There are fewer hours of daylight during the winter. Scientists believe this tells the lemming's brain to produce certain chemicals. These chemicals cause the pigment in the hair to change. White fur begins to grow under the gray fur.

By the time there is snow on the ground, the collared lemming is totally white. When spring comes, the days get longer. This time the collared lemming's fur grows in gray again. This is how the collared lemming stays camouflaged all year long.

27

# Chapter 4 Leaf Me Alone!

There is more unique camouflage in the insect world than in any other group of animals. Perhaps that is because insects are food for so many creatures. Katydids are some of the top "camouflagers" in the entire insect world. That is because they actually look like leaves. If an

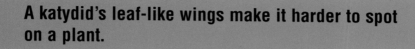

A katydid's leaf-like wings make it harder to spot on a plant.

insect is living and eating in a tree, then looking like a leaf is the best camouflage there is.

Katydids belong to the same group of insects as crickets and grasshoppers. There are hundreds of kinds of katydids all over the world. In North America alone there are more than 200 kinds! They come in many colors, shapes, and sizes. But they all have one thing in common—an awesome ability to camouflage.

## It's Easier Being Green

Like all insects, the body of the katydid has three parts. There is a head, an abdomen, and a thorax. It also has six legs, just like other

**WILD FACT** The Javanese leaf insect is another insect that uses its leaf-like appearance to hide. It even has brown markings to look like an unhealthy leaf! Most animals eat only healthy green leaves. So by looking like a dying leaf, the Javanese leaf insect stays safe.

insects. But unlike those of many other insects, the large bodies of many katydids are bright green and leaf-shaped.

Since being green is not enough to hide the tasty katydid from its predators, its wings actually look like real leaves. Leaves are not completely smooth. Most have veins running down the middle and all over each side. The katydid's wings have the same type of markings. This helps it stay hidden while it eats. Most katydids eat only leaves. They tend

## Wild FACT

Katydid babies are called nymphs. They look very different from adult katydids. They rely on mimicry to avoid predators. Mimicry is an animal's ability to look like something more dangerous or bad-tasting. The animal does not hide, but by looking like something unappealing to predators, it is less likely to get eaten. For example, some types of katydid nymphs look like ants. Many ants can deliver a nasty sting, so birds and other insects avoid eating them.

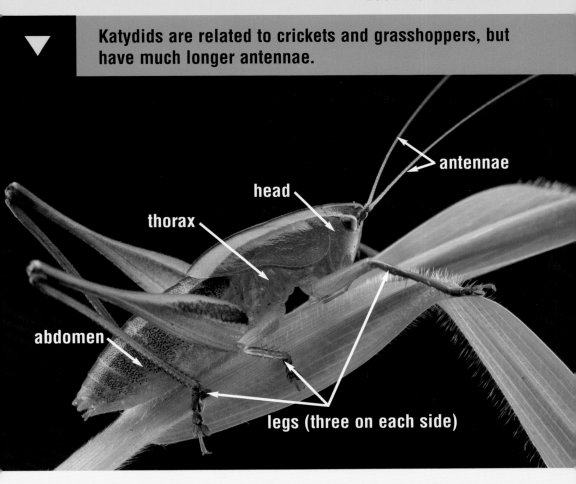

**Katydids are related to crickets and grasshoppers, but have much longer antennae.**

antennae

head

thorax

abdomen

legs (three on each side)

to look like the leaves of whatever plant they find delicious.

While many katydids look like green leaves, there are also brownish katydids. Some have bigger wings than others. Each one has the camouflage that is best for them. They each have the ability to blend in with their own, very

It is easy to see how a predator might overlook this katydid on a dead leaf!

different environments. For example, the lichen katydid has a lacy, white body. Its color and shape perfectly match the spiky, light-colored lichens that it eats. Some katydids have brownish-colored bodies to help them blend in with dead leaves.

## Stickin' It to the Predators

**Not all plants are full of leaves.** Some plants have very few leaves on their branches. Looking like a big green leaf in this type of plant would be very dangerous for an insect. It would offer little protection from hungry birds or other animals. But there is a group of insects that feel safe at home inside a bare tree. They are stick insects!

Stick insects are plant eaters like katydids. Their bodies and legs are long and thin. It is hard to tell one end of a stick insect from the other unless you look closely. There are many different types of stick insects all over the world. The longest is the giant stick insect from South Africa. It can reach up to 13 inches long!

Chapter 5Chapter 5 Screaming Trees

Leaf-tailed geckos are some of the weirdest lizards in the world, and some of the biggest geckos in the world. They can grow to be more than seven inches long. Leaf-tailed geckos also have some of the best camouflage of any reptile.

These geckos can easily hide among piles of dead leaves or on a tree trunk. Some

**Can you see the common leaf-tailed gecko on this tree? Keep looking!**

types have tails that look like brown leaves. The common leaf-tailed gecko of Madagascar is one of the best camouflaged of all the leaf-tailed geckos. It not only has coloring that helps it hide, it has skin that looks like tree bark.

## Its Bark Is Worse Than Its Bite

Like many geckos, the common leaf-tailed gecko is nocturnal. This means that it is active at night. During the day, it sleeps in the jungle trees, flattening itself out on a tree trunk.

## Wild FACT

The common leaf-tailed gecko uses sticky toe pads to hang onto tree trunks—often upside down! Geckos have toe pads that are flat, wide, and covered in small ridges. Every ridge has hundreds of tiny, hooked hairs. On each of those hairs are thousands of smaller hairs. These amazing toes allow geckos to walk almost anywhere—even upside down—without falling.

**A gecko's sticky toes help it stay put on any surface.**

Its rough skin has splotches of light grays and dark browns. This perfectly disguises the gecko as it snoozes in the bark-covered trees. Its sticky toe pads also come in handy since they help hold the gecko on the tree trunk as it rests.

To make its camouflage even better, the common leaf-tailed gecko has dermal (skin) flaps. These are floppy flaps of extra skin on the sides of the gecko's body. The gecko's skin flaps seal off any space between the lizard and the tree trunk that might make a shadow that could be seen by a predator. Predators cannot see where the gecko stops and the tree starts!

Even the gecko's fat, stubby tail lies flat against the tree. The tail of the common

After finding a place to hide (top), a common leaf-tailed gecko uses its dermal flaps to flatten itself against a tree's bark (bottom).

leaf-tailed gecko is where it stores fat. Many geckos have the same type of tail. During times when there is little to eat, the gecko can get energy from the store of fat in its tail.

# Good Pupils

Geckos always seem to be staring, because they never blink! That is because they have no eyelids. Instead, they have a thin, clear membrane that covers the eye. Geckos always have to lick the membrane to keep it clean.

The pupils of the eyes are tiny during the day. They look like thin, vertical lines. At night, the gecko's pupils open wide. This lets in much more light. In fact, the common leaf-tailed gecko has more light-sensitive cells in its eyes than many animals. It needs to be able to see well at night because that is when it hunts for food.

The common leaf-tailed gecko has more teeth than any other land animal. It can have up to 300 teeth in its small mouth! But its bite is not as scary as its "bark." Geckos are the only lizards that can make noise. They can make little noises like barks, chirps, and squeaks. The common leaf-tailed gecko is the loudest of them all, and has a special talent for noise-making.

**Wild FACT** The common leaf-tailed gecko is in danger. There are fewer of them than ever before. Their forest home is being cut down. Many of them are also being taken from their home to be sold as pets. When buying a pet gecko, people should make sure that it is not an endangered species. They should also make sure to buy a gecko only from a well-known pet store.

When frightened, the common leaf-tailed gecko opens its mouth and shows off a bright red tongue. Next, it makes a very shrill, loud noise.

# It's Gecko-man!

**Geckos are famous for climbing.** In Malaysia, there is a gecko that can do more than climb. It can fly!

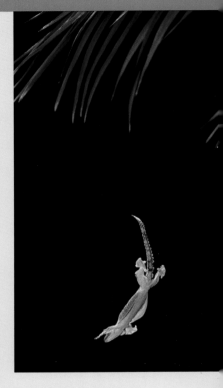

The smooth-backed gliding gecko is no superhero lizard, however. It really just jumps. When it is falling, flaps of skin catch air. Then the gecko floats gently down from tree to tree.

The smooth-backed gliding gecko's skin flaps are a lot like the common leaf-tailed gecko's. They are much bigger, however. As the smooth-backed gliding gecko rests during the day, its skin flaps lie flat against its side. When it jumps, the flaps of skin spread out like wings.

There are five known species of "flying" geckos. They only use their "superpower" to escape danger. These geckos do not fly from place to place like other flying animals. And like most geckos, they try not to be noticed. For the most part, the smooth-backed gliding gecko spends its time like other geckos—dozing in the trees during the day and hunting insects at night.

It sounds much like a loud scream. This scream is why some people in Madagascar are terrified of this lizard. It might not be just the scream that scares people. Since the common leaf-tailed gecko is so well camouflaged, the scream seems to be coming out of a tree trunk!

## Out of Sight, Out of Danger

For the common leaf-tailed gecko and most prey animals, life can be one big game of hide-and-seek. They spend hours each day hiding to keep from being eaten by a predator. Those few animals lucky enough to have their own camouflage are at the top of that hide-and-seek game. The better an animal can blend in with the world around it, the bigger its chances of survival. Whether an animal looks like a leaf, or can change the color of its skin, camouflage is truly an amazing animal defense.

People can learn a lot from animals about how to camouflage themselves. We know that one of the best ways to keep from being hurt or killed is to not be seen. That is one reason people in the armed forces wear camouflaged clothes. These clothes are usually just called "camo."

Soldiers around the world wore colorful uniforms for many years. Bright-colored coats made it easier to recognize fellow soldiers on a crowded battlefield. It also made it easier to spot the enemy. Early in history, a battlefield could be a very smoky place. Cannons and gunpowder were weapons that produced a lot of smoke.

But as weapons improved, there was less smoke during the heat of battle. Without all that smoke cover, the bright-colored clothes stood out in the greens, browns, or even whites of the land. People in the armed forces realized that being seen during a battle was not a good idea, and colorful uniforms were hard to hide. It took a while, but they eventually learned how to hide better.

Most armed forces started wearing colors such as browns and dull greens by the twentieth century. These clothes blended in with the land around them. Today, soldiers can choose from many kinds of camo. What they wear depends on where they are.

Soldiers who are in a snowy area can wear camo that is white and gray. If they are in a sandy desert area, soldiers can wear light brown and khaki uniforms. In forest areas, soldiers wear dark greens

and browns to blend in with the trees. Camo is usually not just one color. It is a pattern of different shades and blotches.

The newest type of camo is called digital camouflage. It uses a smaller dotted color pattern instead of large blotches. These small patterns are much like the pixels of a computer screen. There, tiny squares of color work together to create an image. Digital camo uses that same technology to add what looks like texture in addition to color. This camouflage is thought to be much more realistic looking and better at helping soldiers stay hidden.

# Glossary

**algae**—A group of plant-like, mostly aquatic organisms that lack true roots and stems.

**burrow**—A tunnel-like animal home under the snow or ground.

**camouflage**—When an animal uses its appearance or color to blend in with its surroundings.

**cells**—The tiny, basic structural units of all living things.

**defense**—Protection against an attack.

**habitat**—The area in which an animal lives. A suitable habitat includes enough water, food, space, and shelter.

**hibernate**—To be in a sleep-like, inactive state.

**Industrial Revolution**—A period of time beginning in the late eighteenth century when machines became more commonly used and many factories were built.

**invertebrate**—An animal with no backbone.

**khaki**—A light, sandy-tan color.

**mammal**—An animal with hair or fur. It usually gives birth to live young and is warm blooded. It can also produce milk to feed its young.

**melanin**—A dark pigment produced naturally by skin cells.

**mimicry**—Having the appearance of a more dangerous or bad-tasting animal in order to fool predators.

**nocturnal**—Being active at night and at rest during the day.

**pigment**—Color.

**predator**—An animal that hunts and eats other animals.

**prey**—An animal that is a food source for other animals.

**species**—A group of living things that is very closely related, shares similar characteristics, and can reproduce with one another.

**thorax**—The part of an insect's body between the head and abdomen.

# Further Reading

## Books

Petty, Kate. *Animal Camouflage & Defense.* New York: Chelsea House, 2004.

Squire, Ann O. *Lemmings.* Danbury, Conn.: Children's Press, 2007.

Trueit, Trudi Strain. *Octopuses, Squids, and Cuttlefish.* Danbury, Conn.: Franklin Watts, 2003.

Weber, Belinda. *Animal Disguises.* Boston: Kingfisher Books, 2007.

## Internet Addresses

Camouflage: If You Can't Run, You've Got to Hide!
http://oncampus.richmond.edu/academics/education/projects/webunits/adaptations/camou1.html

Enchanted Learning: Camouflaged Animals
http://www.enchantedlearning.com/coloring/camouflage.shtml

How Stuff Works: How Animal Camouflage Works
http://animals.howstuffworks.com/animal-facts/animal-camouflage.html

# Index